INSIDE THE
NFL

LAS VEGAS
RAIDERS

BY TODD RYAN

SportsZone

An Imprint of Abdo Publishing
abdobooks.com

abdobooks.com

Published by Abdo Publishing, a division of ABDO, PO Box 398166, Minneapolis, Minnesota 55439. Copyright © 2020 by Abdo Consulting Group, Inc. International copyrights reserved in all countries. No part of this book may be reproduced in any form without written permission from the publisher. SportsZone™ is a trademark and logo of Abdo Publishing.

Printed in the United States of America, North Mankato, Minnesota
042019
092019

THIS BOOK CONTAINS
RECYCLED MATERIALS

Cover Photo: Greg Trott/AP Images
Interior Photos: Heinz Kluetmeier/Sports Illustrated/Getty Images, 5, 29; Focus on Sport/Getty Images, 6, 21; Dennis Desprois/Getty Images Sport/Getty Images, 9; Ed Kolenovsky/AP Images, 11; Peter Read Miller/AP Images, 13; Robert Klein/AP Images, 14; Focus on Sport/Getty Images Sport/Getty Images, 17, 30; Charles Aqua Viva/Getty Images Sport/Getty Images, 19; Hall of Fame/AP Images, 23; Fred Kaplan/Sports Illustrated/Getty Images, 25; AP Images, 27, 33, 43; Paul Sakuma/AP Images, 35; Bob Galbraith/AP Images, 36; Kevork Djansezian/AP Images, 39; John Locher/AP Images, 40; Paul Jasienski/AP Images, 41;

Editor: Patrick Donnelly
Series Designer: Craig Hinton

Library of Congress Control Number: 2018965649

Library of Congress Cataloging-in-Publication Data

Names: Ryan, Todd, author.
Title: Las Vegas Raiders / by Todd Ryan
Description: Minneapolis, Minnesota : Abdo Publishing, 2020 | Series: Inside the NFL | Includes online resources and index.
Identifiers: ISBN 9781532118524 (lib. bdg.) | ISBN 9781532172700 (ebook)
Subjects: LCSH: National Football League--Juvenile literature. | Football teams--Juvenile literature. | American football--Juvenile literature.
Classification: DDC 796.33264--dc23

TABLE OF
CONTENTS

CHAPTER 1

FINALLY AT THE TOP

It was the fourth quarter of Super Bowl XI in January 1977. Trailing 26–7, Minnesota Vikings quarterback Fran Tarkenton scanned the field for an open teammate. Tarkenton fired a pass to the left sideline. It was intended for receiver Sammy White.

Willie Brown was the defensive captain of the Oakland Raiders (later to become the Las Vegas Raiders). Brown made sure the pass did not reach its intended target. He cut in front of White and made the interception. Nothing but 75 yards of the Rose Bowl's green grass separated him from sealing Oakland's first National Football League (NFL) championship.

The Raiders' bench exploded to life as Brown raced down the sideline. Camera flashes flickered around stadium.

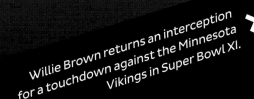

Willie Brown returns an interception for a touchdown against the Minnesota Vikings in Super Bowl XI.

✖ Super Bowl MVP Fred Biletnikoff came up big for the Raiders.

Raiders announcer Bill King emphatically exclaimed, "He's going all the way! . . . Old man Willie!"

With each stride, Brown brought the Raiders closer to fulfilling a dream. Six times in the previous eight seasons, the

Raiders had advanced to within one game of the Super Bowl, only to lose each time to the eventual Super Bowl champion. Brown extended the ball skyward as he crossed the goal line. Within seconds he was mobbed by overjoyed teammates.

The team that could never win the big one just put this game out of reach.

A late Vikings score made the final 32–14. But Super Bowl XI was colored silver and black from the outset. Receiver Fred Biletnikoff caught four timely passes for 79 yards. He was named the game's Most Valuable Player (MVP). Running back Clarence Davis danced and dashed for 137 of the team's 266 rushing yards. Quarterback Ken Stabler completed 12 of 19 passes for 180 yards and a touchdown. Meanwhile, the Oakland defense stood strong throughout.

Raiders coach John Madden had been criticized for not being able to win on the big stage. But on this day, his players carried him off the field. Years later the coach appeared in a special for NFL Films. Madden looked at his Super Bowl ring before focusing squarely on the camera.

"In 1976 we won this ring, and it's always ours," he said. "But bigger than the ring is the memories. You look at it and you remember all those players, and not only the big stars.

A PERFECT FIT

John Madden was known for his wild sideline antics. He was perhaps the perfect coach for the Oakland Raiders. On a team filled with colorful characters, Madden served the role of ringleader with great effectiveness.

The Raiders hired Madden in 1969. In 10 seasons with the team, Madden guided the Raiders to 103 regular-season wins and seven division titles, including five straight from 1972 to 1976. After leaving coaching in 1978, Madden went on to a successful career as a TV commentator. He even lent his name and voice to the Madden NFL video game series. Madden was named to the Pro Football Hall of Fame in 2006.

You remember them all—how they sacrificed. What they did. You earned it. You earned it by playing hard and you earned it by winning. You earned it by being a champion."

The victory in Super Bowl XI was especially important to Madden and the Raiders organization after a string of incredibly frustrating defeats. The year before Madden took over as head coach, the Raiders lost to the New York Jets in the 1968 American Football League (AFL) Championship Game. The next year, the Raiders reached the AFL title game again with their rookie head coach, only to fall to the Kansas City Chiefs. The 10 AFL teams comprised most of the new American Football Conference (AFC) when the AFL and NFL completed their merger in 1970. Oakland made it to the AFC Championship Game that year but lost to the Baltimore Colts.

Raiders players carry John Madden off the field after their Super Bowl victory.

The Raiders continued to have stellar regular seasons. But they could never get over the hump in the playoffs. After missing the playoffs in 1971, Oakland lost to the Pittsburgh Steelers in the first round of the 1972 playoffs. Then the Raiders lost in the AFC Championship Game in three straight years, once to the Miami Dolphins and then twice to the Steelers.

Oakland knew the bitter taste of defeat well. Past failures made the taste of victory for the 1976 team all the sweeter. The Raiders had finally reached their long-elusive goal. They had climbed to the top of the professional football mountain. It was a long journey for a team that almost never existed.

CHAPTER 2

HUMBLE
BEGINNINGS

The AFL played its first season in 1960. The newly formed league was a rival to the long-established NFL. The AFL began with eight teams—the Boston Patriots, Buffalo Bills, Dallas Texans, Denver Broncos, Houston Oilers, Los Angeles Chargers, New York Titans, and Oakland Raiders.

The Raiders almost did not make that list. In fact, they almost did not exist at all. The original eighth member of the AFL was a team that would play in Minnesota. However, the owners of this unnamed team decided to accept an offer to join the NFL instead. That team eventually became the Minnesota Vikings.

The AFL owners scrambled to find a replacement. The city of Oakland, California, was not exactly a prime location.

Raiders fullback Billy Cannon (33) runs through a hole in the Houston Oilers defense during a 1964 game.

THE HEIDI GAME

On November 17, 1968, football on television changed forever. The Raiders were playing in New York when the Jets took a three-point lead with 65 seconds remaining. However, the game had run long. NBC-TV was scheduled to air the children's movie *Heidi* at 7:00 p.m. After the Jets' field goal, NBC aired a commercial and returned with the opening of the movie. Football fans were denied the opportunity to see Oakland rally for the win. Daryle Lamonica threw a touchdown pass to Charlie Smith. Then the Jets fumbled the kickoff and Oakland's Preston Ridlehuber returned it for a touchdown. That finished off a stunning 43–32 victory. Viewers were outraged. After that, the NFL added language to its TV contracts to ensure games are shown in their entirety to the hometown fans.

The rival NFL's San Francisco 49ers were only a few miles away. But Chargers owner Barron Hilton thought that hurdle could be overcome. His team was set to play in Los Angeles. However, the AFL had no other West Coast teams. So Hilton pressured the league to add another team in the West. The AFL eventually agreed and awarded the eighth team to the city of Oakland.

The team's owners were a collection of Oakland businessmen. Their first order of business was to name the team. *Raiders* was not the first pick. In fact, their first name was the Oakland Señors. This name was chosen through a

Center Jim Otto played 15 seasons for the Raiders and was selected to nine AFL All-Star Games and three Pro Bowls.

name-the-team contest. Other names that made the short list included Gauchos, Seawolves, Missiles, and Redwoods. In the end, the name Señors did not stick, and the team was renamed the Raiders before the season started.

Al Davis, *center*, talks with his players during a practice in 1963. Davis was named AFL Coach of the Year that season.

The Raiders' play on the field in those early days was anything but good. Oakland finished its first season with a 6–8 record. However, one of the team's finest players got his start with the Raiders that year—center Jim Otto. He went on to play 15 years for the Raiders. He was enshrined in the Pro Football Hall of Fame in 1980.

JUST WIN, BABY

Al Davis's unusual—some say heavy-handed—way of running the Raiders organization earned him many critics. And he engaged in a series of legal battles throughout his time in Oakland. However, his main passion was always winning.

Some of the phrases he coined include "Just Win, Baby," "Pride and Poise," and "Commitment to Excellence." In fact, Davis even trademarked those slogans.

Davis also lived those words. He often signed other teams' castoffs. He hired whomever he felt gave his team the best chance to win. Skin color and gender never meant anything to Davis. He hired the league's first female CEO, Amy Trask. He hired the first black coach of the modern era, Art Shell. And he hired the first Latino coach, Tom Flores.

Quarterback Tom Flores starred for the Raiders in 1960. He threw for more than 1,700 yards and 12 touchdowns that first season. Flores later became the coach of the Raiders, guiding the team to two Super Bowl victories.

The following two seasons were mostly forgettable. Oakland went 2–12 in 1961 and 1–13 in 1962. The Raiders lost 19 straight games between the two seasons. Things looked bleak in Oakland. Then the team made a bold move. It hired 33-year-old Chargers assistant coach Al Davis to be its new head coach. The Raiders organization was forever changed after that.

With a New York accent and his trademark dark glasses, Davis breathed new life into the franchise. In 1963 the Raiders went 10–4. The team had many stars that season. They included wide receiver Art Powell, running back Clem Daniels, cornerback Fred Williamson, and quarterbacks Flores and Cotton Davidson.

Daniels and Powell were both named first-team All-AFL that season. Daniels ran for more than 1,000 yards. Powell caught 73 passes for 1,304 yards and 16 touchdowns. Davis was named the AFL Coach of the Year. The city of Oakland's love affair with the Raiders had officially begun.

Oakland slumped to 5–7–2 the next season. However, it returned in 1965 with another winning season under Davis. The Raiders had gone 23–16–3 in three seasons under Davis and were no longer the doormats of the league.

Davis left the team in 1966 to become the AFL commissioner. Eight weeks later the AFL and NFL agreed to merge. They would officially become one league in 1970. After the merger, Davis returned to Oakland to run the Raiders. The move triggered a historic run of success rivaled by few teams in any professional sport.

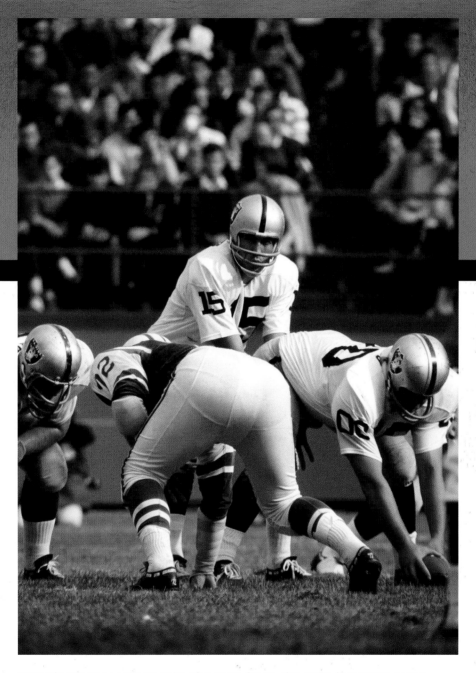

✕ Tom Flores prepares to take the snap from Jim Otto in a 1966 game against the New York Jets.

CHAPTER 3

THE ERA OF SILVER AND BLACK

The Raiders stormed the football world in 1967. They dominated the Denver Broncos 51–0 to open the season. A 35–7 drubbing of the Boston Patriots in Week 2 sent a clear message. The Raiders had arrived. And their image as the AFL's tough guys was gaining steam. With their long-bomb approach on offense and in-your-face style of defense, Oakland was more than formidable.

Behind the strong arm of quarterback Daryle Lamonica, Oakland lit up the scoreboard. The Raiders posted a 13–1 record and their first Western Division title. Lamonica threw for more than 3,000 yards and 30 touchdowns. The Raiders scored at least 40 points in five games. They also rattled off 10 straight wins heading into the AFL Championship Game against the

Quarterback Daryle Lamonica throws a pass against the San Diego Chargers.

Houston Oilers. Lamonica threw two touchdown passes and kicker George Blanda booted four field goals as the Raiders dominated the Oilers 40–7.

The victory propelled the Raiders into Super Bowl II. Despite leading the AFL and NFL with 468 points scored, Oakland could not stand up to the mighty Green Bay Packers. In legendary coach Vince Lombardi's final game with the Packers, Green Bay outmuscled Oakland for a 33–14 victory.

The Super Bowl loss was not a setback for the Raiders, however. Instead, they used it as fuel. Oakland won eight division titles in the next nine years. The Raiders played in many important games during that string of success.

One of the most memorable games for Raiders fans was also one of the most painful. Oakland played the Pittsburgh Steelers in a 1972 divisional playoff game. The game is famous for a play that came to be known as "the Immaculate Reception."

George Blanda (16) and Ken Stabler (12) watch a Blanda field-goal attempt head toward the uprights in 1973.

It was a hard-fought game in Pittsburgh. The defenses dominated all day. Oakland coach John Madden pulled his starting quarterback, Lamonica, and backup Ken Stabler seized the moment. He scampered 30 yards for a touchdown and a 7–6 lead with only 1:13 remaining. It appeared the Raiders had the game in hand. But then the unthinkable happened.

The Steelers needed 10 yards on a fourth-down play at their own 40-yard line with 22 seconds left. Pittsburgh quarterback Terry Bradshaw dropped back to pass. He evaded a heavy rush from Oakland's Horace Jones and Tony Cline. Then he spotted running back Frenchy Fuqua in the middle of the field. Bradshaw fired a pass for Fuqua. Raiders safety Jack Tatum exploded into the Steelers' running back just as the ball arrived. What ensued was simply chaos.

As Tatum slammed into Fuqua, the ball ricocheted back toward the line of scrimmage. Steelers running back Franco Harris made a shoestring catch and galloped down the left sideline. Bewildered Raiders gave chase in vain. As Harris crossed the goal line for the victory, the shocked crowd at Three Rivers Stadium erupted. So did Madden and the Raiders players.

The rules at the time prohibited a player from catching a pass that deflected directly off a teammate. The question remained whether it was Tatum or Fuqua who had touched the ball before Harris caught it. The referees eventually

KINGS OF MONDAY NIGHT

Few NFL teams ever thrived in the spotlight of *Monday Night Football* the way the Raiders did from 1970 through 1985. During that time, the team posted an incredible 24–3–1 record when playing on Monday night.

John Madden, *top center*, and numerous players swarm officials who are deciding whether Pittsburgh running back Franco Harris's "Immaculate Reception" should stand.

decided the play should stand. The defeated Raiders were in disbelief.

"They said it was my deflection, but I've seen the films and I still can't tell," Tatum said years later. "I wish we could have played the Steelers 16 times a season. Those were always such great games."

Two years later, the Raiders found themselves in another game for the ages. This time they came out on top. Oakland hosted the two-time defending NFL champion Miami Dolphins in the divisional round of the playoffs. It was a back-and-forth

THE HOLY ROLLER

On September 10, 1978, the Raiders were involved in another of the NFL's zaniest plays. Oakland trailed the San Diego Chargers 20–14 with 10 seconds left. Quarterback Ken Stabler dropped to pass. He was about to be sacked. In desperation, he fumbled the ball forward. Running back Pete Banaszak approached the ball around the 10-yard line and also flung it forward. Finally, tight end Dave Casper batted the ball around, kicking it once, before falling on it in the end zone for the winning touchdown.

The Chargers were outraged. The play eventually led to a rule change. Now, during the final two minutes of the half or regulation, only the fumbling player can advance a fumble.

contest that featured six lead changes. The Raiders took the lead with 4:37 left when Stabler hit wide receiver Cliff Branch on a long bomb to the Miami 27-yard line. Although Branch fell to the ground, no Dolphins player touched him. Branch got up and scampered to the end zone to complete a 72-yard touchdown. That gave the Raiders a 21–19 lead. But the lead did not last. The Dolphins responded with a 23-yard touchdown run by Benny Malone with 2:08 left. There was just enough time for one frantic drive into history.

Stabler completed a series of passes to move the Raiders into scoring position. Fred Biletnikoff made three critical catches on the drive. The Raiders had the ball on the Dolphins' 8-yard line with only seconds remaining. Stabler dropped back

Clarence Davis (28) comes down with the ball in the end zone to score the game-winning touchdown in the "Sea of Hands" game.

to pass. He looked for Biletnikoff, who was covered. Stabler then scrambled to his left. As he was being tackled from behind, he hurled the ball toward Clarence Davis and three Miami players. Somehow, Davis ripped the ball away from the defenders for the winning touchdown. Fittingly, the victory is referred to as the "Sea of Hands" game.

CHAPTER 4

AGAINST ALL ODDS

In 1980 the Oakland Raiders did not have the look of a champion. In the fifth game of the season, starting quarterback Dan Pastorini suffered a broken leg. The Raiders called on 33-year-old castoff Jim Plunkett. Plunkett promptly threw five interceptions in a 31–17 loss to the Kansas City Chiefs. Oakland slumped to 2–3.

The Raiders always believed in second chances. Plunkett had been a Heisman Trophy winner at Stanford University. But he had struggled throughout his professional career to that point. This was his chance. And he didn't miss his shot.

Plunkett led the Raiders on a historic march. The team won nine of its 11 remaining games. The Raiders even secured a wild-card spot in the playoffs. No wild-card team

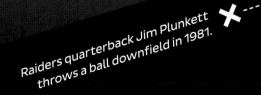

Raiders quarterback Jim Plunkett throws a ball downfield in 1981.

ANOTHER CHANCE

Expectations were high for quarterback Jim Plunkett when he came out of college. The New England Patriots drafted him number one overall in 1971. But he played five mostly forgettable seasons with the Patriots. He then played two more mediocre years with the San Francisco 49ers.

In 1978 he signed with the Raiders. Plunkett's career was widely considered a bust at that point. He saw very little action during his first two seasons. But then he took over after starter Dan Pastorini was injured. Once he got the job, he did not let go until injuries derailed his career. Plunkett led the Raiders to two Super Bowl victories. He is the only eligible starting quarterback in league history with two Super Bowl victories who isn't in the Pro Football Hall of Fame.

had ever won the Super Bowl before. The Raiders went about changing that. They advanced after drubbing the Houston Oilers 27–7 in the AFC Wild Card Game. The next week, it appeared Oakland's season might end on an ice-covered field in Cleveland. The Raiders led the Browns 14–12. But Cleveland's offense was on the move late in the game. Behind quarterback Brian Sipe, the Browns marched to the Oakland 13 with less than a minute to play.

All Cleveland needed was a field goal. But the icy conditions made that no guarantee. Also on the Browns' minds was the fact that 6-foot-7 Ted Hendricks had blocked an extra point earlier in the game. The Browns decided to throw a pass into

Oakland safety Mike Davis makes a game-saving interception in the Raiders' playoff victory at Cleveland in January 1981.

the end zone, hoping to catch Oakland by surprise. But safety Mike Davis wasn't fooled. He stepped in front of tight end Ozzie Newsome and made an interception to seal the victory.

The next week, Oakland played its third straight road playoff game. The Raiders traveled to San Diego for the AFC Championship Game. Plunkett threw touchdown passes to Raymond Chester and Kenny King. He ran for another—all in the first quarter. The Chargers rallied, but the Raiders held on to win 34–27. The victory set up a Super Bowl showdown

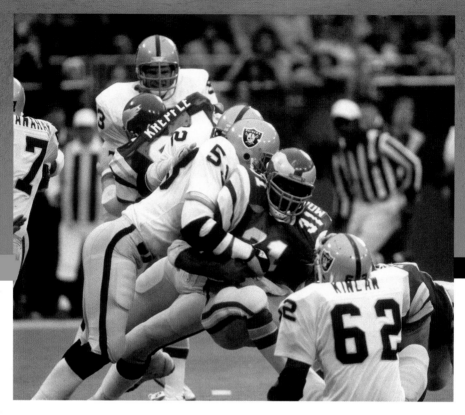

The Raiders defense wraps up Philadelphia Eagles running back Wilbert Montgomery in Super Bowl XV.

against the Philadelphia Eagles. The Eagles had already defeated the Raiders 10–7 earlier in the season.

But Super Bowl XV was a rout. Plunkett threw three touchdown passes, including two to Cliff Branch, and was named Super Bowl MVP. Oakland linebacker Rod Martin was another candidate. He intercepted Eagles quarterback Ron Jaworski three times.

The Raiders had done what no other football team had done before. They won the Super Bowl as a wild-card team, bucking all odds. They were on top of the football world again. But not long after, in 1982, they headed south. Al Davis, who had become the team's majority owner in the early 1970s, won a lengthy legal battle with the NFL. He moved the Raiders from Oakland to Los Angeles. The question was whether their winning ways would make the move with them.

The Raiders' second season in Los Angeles was in 1983. All the pieces were in place for another run at the championship. Plunkett was the team's established leader at quarterback. Running back Marcus Allen was quickly becoming one of the league's best. Tight end Todd Christensen was nearly unstoppable, too. He made first-team All-Pro that season with 92 catches for 1,247 yards and 12 touchdowns.

The Raiders averaged more than 27 points per game. They roared into the playoffs as AFC West champs with a 12–4 record. In the playoffs, Los Angeles kept rolling with easy wins over the Pittsburgh Steelers and Seattle Seahawks.

Next up was Super Bowl XVIII against Washington, which had scored a then-NFL record 541 points that season. Even the most dedicated Raiders fans could not see what was to come.

The Raiders dominated from start to finish. Allen ran for a then–Super Bowl record 191 yards and two touchdowns. He also made the game's signature play in the third quarter. Allen took a handoff and navigated to his left only to find the path blocked. He quickly reversed his direction and eluded tacklers until he found a crack. He then shot through the Washington defense and sprinted 74 yards for a touchdown.

While Allen's play is the game's signature moment, a play just before halftime might have been its most crucial. With 12 seconds left in the half, Washington's Joe Theismann tried to throw a screen pass. Instead, Oakland linebacker Jack Squirek intercepted the ball and returned it 5 yards for a touchdown to

Marcus Allen had the Washington defense tied in knots throughout Super Bowl XVIII.

give the Raiders a 21–3 halftime lead. The Raiders cruised to a 38–9 victory and their third Super Bowl title.

The Raiders made the playoffs the following two years, but the magic in Los Angeles soon faded. From 1986 to 1994, the team won 10 games or more only twice. In 1995 Al Davis again shocked the football world by moving his club back to its original home in Oakland. The glory years in Oakland were far removed, though. The team had a lot of work to do to right the ship.

CHAPTER 5

ON THE
MOVE AGAIN

Back in Oakland, the Raiders did not return to their winning ways immediately. Coach Art Shell was fired before the team made the move from Los Angeles. Mike White and Joe Bugel failed to post winning records. The arrival of Jon Gruden in 1998 helped turn the team around.

The Raiders went 8–8 in 1998 and 1999. Gruden's short, controlled passing attack meshed well with quarterback Rich Gannon. The team won back-to-back division titles in 2000 and 2001.

Adding to their long list of controversies, the Raiders came out on the wrong side of a game now known as the "Tuck Rule Game." In January 2002, Oakland played a playoff game at New England. The Raiders led 13–10 as the Patriots

Oakland's passionate fans welcomed the Raiders back to town in 1995.

✖ The Raiders thrived under fiery young head coach Jon Gruden.

drove down the field late in the game. Raiders cornerback Charles Woodson blitzed Patriots quarterback Tom Brady, hitting him hard and jarring the ball free. Oakland's Greg Biekert pounced on the ball, seemingly ending the game.

Instead, the referees ruled that Brady had started to throw a pass but stopped without tucking the ball back into his body. So, the play was an incomplete pass under the so-called "tuck rule." New England went on to win in overtime.

The heartbreaking loss was the last one under Gruden. Al Davis clashed with the brash young coach and traded him to the Tampa Bay Buccaneers in exchange for four draft picks. The Raiders' offensive coordinator, Bill Callahan, took over.

The Raiders didn't miss a beat. They won the AFC West for the third year in a row and Gannon was league MVP. They made it all the way to Super Bowl XXXVII. It was the team's fifth Super Bowl appearance. The face on the other sideline was familiar. It was Gruden, who had led the Buccaneers to a conference title in his first year in Tampa Bay.

The highlight of the game for Oakland was taking a 3–0 lead in the first quarter. It was all downhill from there. The normally reliable Gannon threw five interceptions as the Raiders were totally dominated. Gruden had the last laugh with a 48–21 victory.

What followed was the worst era in Raiders history. From 2003 to 2015, the Raiders failed to record a winning season.

MR. RAIDER

Tim Brown's magnificent career with the Silver and Black earned him the nickname "Mr. Raider." The Heisman Trophy winner out of Notre Dame played 16 seasons with the Raiders, from 1988 to 2003, and was a nine-time Pro Bowler. He played one final season with Tampa Bay. Brown's 240 games with the Raiders are a team best. He also holds nearly every team receiving record. As a Raider, Brown caught 1,070 passes for 14,734 yards and 99 touchdowns.

They changed head coaches eight times. High draft picks didn't work out.

And for the first time in its history, the Raiders were under new management. Longtime owner Al Davis died in 2011. That left his son, Mark Davis, in charge of the franchise.

The Raiders' resurgence started with finally finding a quarterback. They drafted Fresno State's Derek Carr in the second round in 2014 and he immediately earned the starting job. After going 3–13 his first season, Carr led the Raiders to seven wins and earned a trip to the Pro Bowl with 32 touchdown passes in 2015. The next season, the Raiders went 12–4 and made the playoffs for the first time in 14 years. Carr threw for 28 touchdowns and only six interceptions.

The Raiders' on-field future looked bright. But it was cloudy off the field. For years, the Davis family tried to get a new

✕ Tim Brown breaks loose for a touchdown against the Chargers.

stadium built on Oakland. When nothing developed, the team started to look elsewhere.

In 2016 the Raiders tried to get approval to move to Carson, California, near Los Angeles. But the move was voted down by the other NFL owners. Mark Davis began looking to Las Vegas. After the city agreed to a proposal to finance a new stadium, the Raiders asked the league to move.

The relocation was approved by a 31–1 vote in March 2017. For the third time in their history, the Raiders were on the move. Later that year near the famous Las Vegas Strip,

Football fans in Las Vegas welcomed the Raiders to their new home.

construction began on a new domed stadium with room for 65,000 fans. But the new stadium was not going to be ready until 2020. They had three more seasons to play in Oakland.

Unfortunately, they were not memorable final seasons for Raiders fans. Oakland went 6–10 in 2017 and missed the playoffs. Mark Davis brought back Gruden, who had been a broadcaster since leaving Tampa Bay in 2008. Then before the 2018 season started, the team traded away Defensive Player of

× The Raiders' new stadium in Las Vegas began to take shape as their move-in date drew near.

the Year Khalil Mack. The Raiders lost eight of their first nine games en route to a 4–12 season.

The move to Las Vegas symbolized a fresh start for the team. It was a difficult decision for the fans in Oakland to accept. But many of them had stuck with their Raiders through earlier moves. Those who remained Silver-and-Black diehards just hoped the team could get back to competing for Super Bowls, even in a new state.

TIMELINE

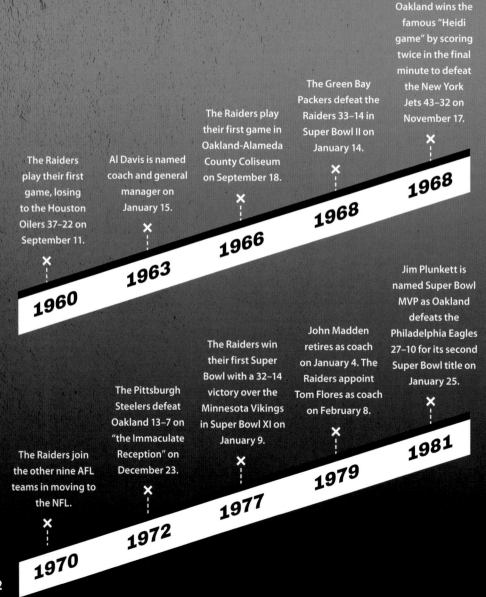

Oakland wins the famous "Heidi game" by scoring twice in the final minute to defeat the New York Jets 43–32 on November 17.

The Green Bay Packers defeat the Raiders 33–14 in Super Bowl II on January 14.

The Raiders play their first game in Oakland-Alameda County Coliseum on September 18.

Al Davis is named coach and general manager on January 15.

The Raiders play their first game, losing to the Houston Oilers 37–22 on September 11.

1960

1963

1966

1968

1968

Jim Plunkett is named Super Bowl MVP as Oakland defeats the Philadelphia Eagles 27–10 for its second Super Bowl title on January 25.

John Madden retires as coach on January 4. The Raiders appoint Tom Flores as coach on February 8.

The Raiders win their first Super Bowl with a 32–14 victory over the Minnesota Vikings in Super Bowl XI on January 9.

The Pittsburgh Steelers defeat Oakland 13–7 on "the Immaculate Reception" on December 23.

The Raiders join the other nine AFL teams in moving to the NFL.

1970

1972

1977

1979

1981

The Raiders move from Oakland to Los Angeles. They defeat the San Diego Chargers 28–24 in their first home game in Los Angeles.

Marcus Allen runs for a record 191 yards and is named the game's MVP as the Raiders defeat Washington 38–9 in Super Bowl XVIII on January 22.

The Raiders sign an agreement on August 7 to return to Oakland.

The Raiders lose to the New England Patriots in the "Tuck Rule" game on January 19.

Quarterback Rich Gannon wins the NFL MVP Award after passing for a franchise-record 4,689 yards.

1982

1984

1995

2002

2002

The Raiders fall to the Tampa Buccaneers 48–21 in Super Bowl XXXVII on January 26.

Longtime owner Al Davis dies at the age of 82.

The Raiders announce on March 27 that they intend to move to Las Vegas for the 2020 season.

Jon Gruden is re-hired as head coach on January 6.

The Raiders lose eight of their first nine games and finish 4–12 in Gruden's first year back with the team.

2003

2011

2017

2018

2018

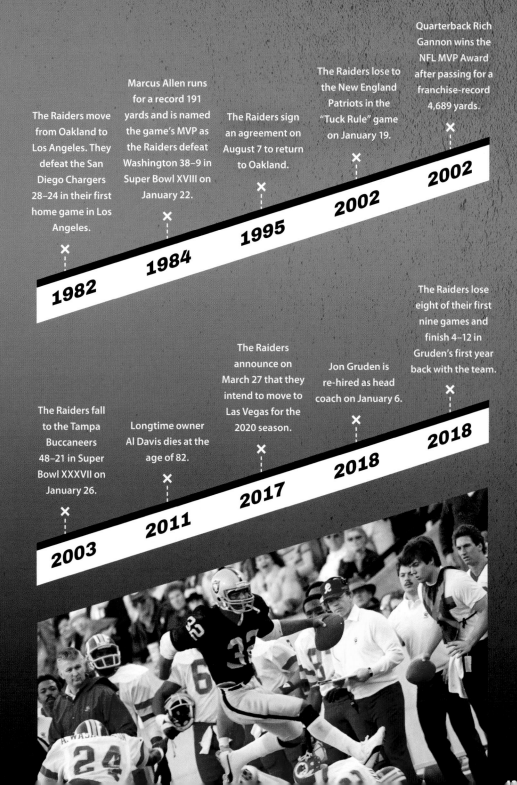

QUICK STATS

FRANCHISE HISTORY

Oakland Raiders (AFL) 1960–69
Oakland Raiders (NFL) 1970–81;
  1995–2019
Los Angeles Raiders 1982–94
Las Vegas Raiders 2020–

SUPER BOWLS *(wins in bold)*

1967 (II), **1976 (XI)**, **1980 (XV)**,
1983 (XVIII), 2002 (XXXVII)

AFL CHAMPIONSHIP GAMES *(1960–69, wins in bold)*

1967, 1968, 1969

AFC CHAMPIONSHIP GAMES *(since 1970 AFL-NFL merger)*

1970, 1973, 1974, 1975, 1976, 1977,
1980, 1983, 1990, 2000, 2002

KEY COACHES

Tom Flores (1979–1987):
  83–53, 8–3 (playoffs)
John Madden (1969–1978):
  103–32–7, 9–7 (playoffs)

KEY PLAYERS *(position, seasons with team)*

Marcus Allen (RB, 1982–92)
Fred Biletnikoff (WR, 1965–78)
George Blanda (QB/K, 1967–75)
Tim Brown (WR, 1988–2003)
Willie Brown (DB, 1967–78)
Derek Carr (QB, 2014–)
Dave Casper (TE, 1974–80, 1984)
Ted Hendricks (LB, 1975–83)
Howie Long (DE, 1981–93)
Jim Otto (C, 1960–74)
Jim Plunkett (QB, 1979–86)
Art Shell (T, 1968–82)
Ken Stabler (QB, 1968–79)
Jack Tatum (S, 1971–79)
Gene Upshaw (G, 1967–81)

HOME FIELDS

Las Vegas Stadium (2020–)
Oakland-Alameda County
  Coliseum (1966–81; 1995–2019)
Los Angeles Memorial Coliseum
  (1982–94)
Frank Youell Field (1962–65)
Candlestick Park (1960–61)
Kezar Stadium (1960)

*All statistics through 2018 season

Perhaps no player in the 1960s better portrayed the Raiders' image than defensive end "Big" Ben Davidson. He stood 6 feet 8 inches and sported a fierce handlebar mustache. He also played with unrelenting passion. Davidson terrorized opposing quarterbacks for the Raiders from 1964 to 1971. One particular incident is often replayed when the Raiders face the Chiefs. In 1970 Kansas City appeared to have victory in hand when quarterback Len Dawson ran for a late-game first down. Davidson lunged on top of Dawson and was flagged for spearing. The Chiefs retaliated for what they deemed a dirty play. The ensuing fight resulted in offsetting penalties and negated the play. The Chiefs eventually had to punt, and Oakland rallied for the tying field goal. Davidson was a three-time AFL All-Star and made first-team all-AFL once.

"If my mother put on a helmet and shoulder pads and a uniform that wasn't the same as the one I was wearing, I'd run over her if she was in my way. And I love my mother."

—Bo Jackson on his competitive streak

"We want to win. The Raider fans deserve it. The Raider players deserve it, even my organization deserves it. You have to win and you have to win with a vision for the Super Bowl. That's our passion here."

—Al Davis on his personal philosophy for running the Raiders

"I don't know how we should feel. I feel the pain of our fans in Oakland. I also see the joy on the faces of our new fans in Las Vegas. As players, we will show up and give everything we have. We will compete, and we will do our best to bring a championship to the entire Raider Nation."

—Derek Carr upon hearing that the team planned to move to Las Vegas

GLOSSARY

blitz
When a linebacker or defensive back attacks the line of scrimmage to stop a run or sack the quarterback.

commissioner
The chief executive of a sports league.

coordinator
An assistant coach who is in charge of the offense or defense.

cornerback
A defensive player who normally covers wide receivers.

draft
A system that allows teams to acquire new players coming into a league.

franchise
A sports organization, including the top-level team and all minor league affiliates.

goal line
The edge of the end zone that a player must cross with the ball to score a touchdown.

Hall of Fame
The highest honor a player or coach can get when his or her career is over.

merge
Join with another to create something new, such as a company, a team, or a league.

Pro Bowl
The NFL's all-star game, in which the best players in the league compete.

MORE INFORMATION

BOOKS

Cohn, Nate. *Oakland Raiders*. New York: AV2 by Weigl, 2018.

Kelley, Patrick. *Oakland Raiders*. Minneapolis, MN: Abdo Publishing, 2017.

Zappa, Marcia. *Oakland Raiders*. Minneapolis, MN: Abdo Publishing, 2015.

ONLINE RESOURCES

Booklinks
NONFICTION NETWORK
FREE! ONLINE NONFICTION RESOURCES

To learn more about the Las Vegas Raiders, visit
abdobooklinks.com or scan this QR code. These links are
routinely monitored and updated to provide the most current
information available.

PLACES TO VISIT

Las Vegas Stadium
3333 Al Davis Way
Paradise, NV 89118
lasvegasstadium.raiders.com

The Raiders' new home in Las Vegas is located near the airport and the
famous Las Vegas Strip, making it an ideal spot for out-of-town fans to visit.

Pro Football Hall of Fame
2121 George Halas Dr. N
Canton, OH 44708
330–456–8207
profootballhof.com

This hall of fame and museum highlights the greatest players and moments in
the history of the AFL and NFL.

INDEX

ABOUT THE AUTHOR

Todd Ryan is a library assistant from the Upper Peninsula of Michigan. He lives near Houghton with his two cats, Izzo and Mooch.